King Solomon's Thirty Tips on How to Prophesy

Ben Emet

Published by

An Imprint of Melrose Press Limited
St Thomas Place, Ely
Cambridgeshire
CB7 4GG, UK
www.melrosebooks.co.uk

FIRST EDITION

Copyright © Ben Emet 2018

The Author asserts his moral right to
be identified as the author of this work

Cover by Melrose Books

ISBN   978-1-912333-66-0 Paperback
       978-1-912333-67-7 ePub
       978-1-912333-68-4 Mobi

All rights reserved. No part of this publication may be reproduced, stored in a retrieval system, or transmitted, in any form or by any means electronic, mechanical, photocopying, recording or otherwise, without the prior permission of the publishers.

This book is sold subject to the condition that it shall not, by way of trade or otherwise, be lent, re-sold, hired out or otherwise circulated without the publisher's prior consent in any form of binding or cover other than that in which it is published and without a similar condition including this condition being imposed on the subsequent purchaser.

Printed and bound in Great Britain by:
CMP (UK) Ltd, G3 The Fulcrum, Vantage Way
Poole, Dorset, BH12 4NU

Scripture references are from the following sources:
The Holy Bible: New King James Version © 1982 by Thomas Nelson, Inc. English Standard Version © 2010 by Crossway. New American Standard Bible © 1960, 1962, 1963, 1968, 1971, 1972, 1973, 1975, 1977, 1995 by The Lockman Foundation. New International Version © 1973, 1978, 1984 by Biblica, Inc. The Amplified Bible, Expanded Edition © 1987 by Zondervan and The Lockman Foundation. The Complete Jewish Bible © 1998 by Jewish New Testament Publications, Inc. The Living Bible © 2005 by Tyndale House Publishers, Inc. Good News Bible © 1976 by American Bible Society. The Message © 1993, 1994, 1995 by NavPress.

Contents

Introduction	vii
Day 1: Thirty principles on how to be prophetic!	1
Day 2: First tip: it's a responsible assignment, but rewarding	4
Day 3: Prophecy: merciful, gracious, slow to anger	7
Day 4: Of myself I cannot say or do anything	10
Day 5: Establishing boundaries as God willed it	13
Day 6: And then you'll stand before kings …	16
Day 7: Entertain God's guests and serve them well	19
Day 8: My Beloved is mine and I am His	22
Day 9: Bless others without any hidden motives	25
Day 10: A time to speak forth and a time to be quiet	28
Day 11: Stand with God as He fights for the fatherless	31
Day 12: Don't refuse criticism; get all the help you can	34
Day 13: As His child, submit to His hand of correction	37
Day 14: Born to speak at such a time as this	40
Day 15: Having done all, enabled to stand with Him (Eph. 6:13)	43
Day 16: Stay on course and don't get distracted	46
Day 17: Honour your father and mother …	49
Day 18: By grace, purchase God's eternal blessings	52
Day 19: Get into the divine cycle of love	55
Day 20: With joy, drink deeply from God's fountain	58
Day 21: His wine is always better than anything else	61
Day 22: Choose your friends well, and ask for God's help	64
Day 23: Jesus is our firm foundation	67
Day 24: Father will give you His Counsellor, His aide	70

Day 25: A fool can't be a counsellor; he lacks wisdom	73
Day 26: It's His plan, in His time and in His way	76
Day 27: Weak in a crisis? Weak indeed!	79
Day 28: Speak up, there's no excuse!	82
Day 29: Plans to give you a future and a hope	85
Day 30: Prophecy shouldn't bring ruin; rather, new life	88
Day 31: Don't judge, lest you be judged	91
Day 32: Don't look around, say what you have to say	94
Day 33: Respect God's delegated authority	97
Epilogue	100
Bibliography	101

Introduction

We often use Psalms to pray or speak to God, but He uses Proverbs to speak to us, and as a Father He addressed it to 'His son' more than twenty times. So, these are principles that transcend the literal and practical wisdoms, even though they are also included. We must look past the obvious and discern the eternal. How do these 'wise sayings' draw us closer to God our Father? How does understanding His mind by these sayings transform the way we walk with Him and communicate with each other, now, as well as eternally?

Solomon was and will be the wisest man ever alive; it's a promise God made him. We must avoid confusing wisdom with godly character or maturity, and although they're not mutually exclusive, they're not the same either. Even though Solomon eventually strayed off God's chosen path, it didn't negate the wisdom that God gave him; he still had a thorough understanding of God's nature, mind and plans. Perhaps we should approach the book without that subtle prejudice and see it as fully God-inspired, as *He* moved the wisest author that ever lived.

Now for the crucial bit. When we read Prov. 22:20, the Father says to His son, "Have I not written for you thirty sayings of counsel and knowledge, to make you know what is right and true, that you may give a true answer to those who sent you?" It is important to picture this scene. The son here is an intercessor, asking on behalf of others who had sent him to the Father, to enquire from Him and to return with a godly answer, to speak the mind of God on the matter. That, in essence, is **prophecy**; the ability to speak the word in season, as God determines. Here we receive thirty principles on how to prophesy. Each and every one of us, as sons or children of God, needs to be able to stand in the gap for one other; to edify, exhort and comfort each other according to God's mind and will (1 Cor. 14:3).

Aims:

Proverbs 22–24 contains thirty lessons in how to prophesy. My aims in expounding these principles encapsulated in these thirty sayings were manifold:

1. To reflect the spiritual or eternal perspective *more* than the obvious literal meaning.
2. To respond to the prompting of "His word of faith". As you read this devotional it will change the way you look at things. As Father-God speaks to us, these words help us to understand how to prophesy in line with His heart or mind. These principles aren't rigid; they are guidance to keep you and the recipients safe, just as He promised, "that you may give a true answer to those who sent you".
3. To lead the reader into a prophetic mindset. To make him or her hungry to hear from God themselves and to start speaking the mind of God. To clarify these sayings for those who earnestly desire the best spiritual gifts.
4. To tune into the flow of what Holy Spirit was saying at that *and* this time. This might seem personal, and it is, but the truth emanating from those revelations was at times very fresh and challenging. I have no doubt that whoever reads and

uses the book will learn a lot on how to prophesy and have a lot of fun along the way!
5. To deliver these truths in daily, bite sizes, as a devotional Bible study. Sound hermeneutical (interpreting) principles were kept in hand. Quite a bit of terminology is explained along the way to help the reader adopt the ideas behind some Hebrew words and their usage.
6. To inspire the reader *to fall in love with the book and its Author* and to grow in his or her own spiritual walk as they go along.
7. To use simple language, yet also include meatier theological bits to bring out the deeper understanding of the text or meaning of the words and the proverb.
8. To teach believers the "language of God". Regardless of what people might say, in Scripture, the LORD is consistent with His symbols and what they represent. Holy Spirit will activate God's language by means of use, and in time will become easier to follow and understand.

Keys in understanding Proverbs

One of the crucial keys in understanding the book of Proverbs is the way people are represented in the book. It is of the utmost importance to understand that any one of us can fall into any of the "bad" or "good" categories. This is where the literalist approach falls short. Proverbs recognises that in our daily living we can all become "foolish", or "act wickedly", or do the "right" things. It does not change the fact that you have been made righteous in Christ Jesus, it just identifies you with what best describes you *for that moment* or *season*, with what the proverb is declaring for that time. Father wants to give us insight and understanding into His mind and how His kingdom works; and so, to keep it simple, the particular sin is personified; it's not to label one's identity, but to emphasise the principle at work. To exhort us one way or another when we choose to follow that particular route.

For instance, "the simple" are those who can only cope with one thing at a time (which could include babes in Christ), not being able to handle the meatier aspects of God's wisdom. The "fool" is not only the person who says "there is no God", it's whenever a person lives or acts instinctively without recognising God, or acknowledging Him in any given situation. In Proverbs, for that moment, one has become "a fool". The "wicked" are those who know what the right thing is to do, but choose not to do so, for whatever selfish reason; which in turn is very different from the "sluggard" or lazy person, being people who are complacent, unwilling to move as God desires (non-Christian or Christian – happy with the old wine only!). The "righteous" are those who desire to walk with God and the "wise" are those who walk in harmony with God's will and plans and who fully embrace Jesus through Holy Spirit.

Revealing God's heart and mind

As we walk through these sayings, the heart and mind of Father-God is revealed more and more; His desires and specific dislikes. Also, bear in mind it's written from the eternal perspective, because it's addressed to the "son", therefore it's not about "salvation" per se; rather, it's about "reflecting God's righteousness" and producing the fruit of "right living", learning to adopt a righteous lifestyle. It is about transforming our minds and thinking to understand the will and mind of God. Proverbs will cut to the heart probably more than any other

Biblical book, for it is based on Father-God's instructions to us, His children.

There is a danger here: the process is not to introduce any kind of legalism, but to recognise God and His principles, instilling a reverential awe, honour and deep love for Him. Every principle has grace at its foundation; never lose that truth as you study these sayings.

The concepts or Spirit behind these principles
If we are talking about the mind of God, then we must consider the fact that as with the Law there are the literal laws; but the "spirit" of the Law which Jesus brought to light in the Sermon on the Mount is more important. We are called to discern the spiritual implications and applications in proverbs and not just read things at face value alone. And these hold true for prophecy, for we want to impart the love, goodness and destiny of God on to those who receive our prophecies.

Methods and Bibles used
Initially two and later three translations were used, as well as three paraphrases; to construct a compound proverb (combining them) and so get a basic and general understanding of the relevant context and/or concepts. Call it a comparative integrated approach. A bit like a stew with all the Bibles involved, not giving special preference to any one specifically, but rather to combine them to get the clearest understanding across.

That might make smooth reading more difficult and it will come across a little strange and demanding at first, but as you get used to the format it will help the reader to get the most out of the proverb. This also helps to demonstrate not only the difficulties faced by the translators to get the "right" word, but it also demonstrates how obscure some passages in

Proverbs can appear in their original languages. My advice is to reflect on these different words. That alone can be inspirational, seeing how the concepts are woven into a picture telling us just how great our God is, but from different angles using different words.

Proverbs contains object lessons from God
The Hebrew title for Proverbs is *Mishlei*, which in its most basic sense means, "to compare with" and/or "to rule", but is generally taken to mean "a pithy (terse) saying, especially one condensing the wisdom of God's mind as seen through experience". Thus, they are object lessons from life, as God intends it, to impart direction and godly thinking even as you speak out on His behalf.

The idea is for "a proverb a day", and on the whole, that was achieved. There were two proverbs that needed two days each for better clarification!

Should you choose to use this book, you will be challenged at times, but also, continually drawn closer to God in your relationship with Him, and you will be encouraged and exhorted to speak forth the mind of God, that is, to prophesy!

Layout:
The readings for each day are set out as follows:
1. The proverb(s) quoted in a parallel integrated fashion.
2. The devotional exposition and homily.
3. A concluding prayer.

The abbreviations accepted for each translation are as follows:

NKJV – New King James Version
NASB – New American Standard Bible
ESV – English Standard Version
AMP – The Amplified Expanded Edition
CJB – Complete Jewish Bible
NIV – New International Version
NLT – New Living Translation
GN – Good News Bible
TM – The Message

The journaling space could not be standardised as the devotional message for each day differed, but it could be of great use if the reader chooses to use the space for their own notes.

Day 1
Thirty principles on how to be prophetic!

> That your trust may be in the LORD, I have made them known to you today, even to you. Have I not written for you thirty sayings of counsel (advice) and knowledge, to make you know what is right and true, that you may give a true answer (take an accurate report) to those who sent you? TM: To make sure your foundation is trust in God, I'm laying it all out right now just for you. I'm giving you thirty sterling principles – tested guidelines to live by. Believe me – these are truths that work, and will keep you accountable to those who sent you.

This is incredible. In plain English it says, "If you'll take everything on board, these thirty principles that I am teaching you, today, and make them your own, they will give you discernment *and help you to speak My will in an accountable way to all those who ask you for godly advice* (for they sent you to Me to get a word for them). For a second time we see that God wants us not only to be prophetic, but to do so in an accountable way, so He gave us a set of principles to help us to get good at it. Wow! When the proverb says "today", it is set the timeless "now", tomorrow is the next "today", in other words, every day He'll instruct you to get better at being His spokesperson (mouthpiece). It stresses "even you", yes, you! Because it's personal! You now know, you've been told, you've been designated. The reader is the recipient of His word, daily, in season for those who have asked for a word from God. Re. 3:16 affirms that we are all called to be God's mouthpiece – let him who has an ear, hear! Called to speak words of exhortation (giving proper direction), edification (encouragement, promoting spiritual growth) and comfort (bringing God's consolation). Paul said that he would not dare to speak of anything else than what God had accomplished in his life, in word and deed. And, if we are going to be a royal priesthood, how can we fulfil our duties if we do not listen to the King? We have His written word, but we speak forth His spoken word. We are to be reliable ambassadors and deliver God's messages in an accountable and responsible way. What an honour and privilege.

Almighty God and heavenly Father, Lord Jesus Christ, Holy Spirit; help me to listen very carefully to the sayings You want to impart to me. Give me Your words daily and help me to faithfully pass them on as You would want me to, in Jesus' name, amen.

*O*wn notes:

Day 2

First tip: it's a responsible assignment, but rewarding

> Do not rob (exploit, tear from) the poor because he is poor, or crush the afflicted (needy) at the gate (in court). For the LORD will plead their case and take the life of those who rob them. Don't take advantage of the poor just because you can; don't take advantage of those who stand helpless in court. The LORD will argue their case for them and the life you took; he'll take from you and give back to them.

The first principle is to understand how God sees the "poor", the one who is in need of His word. Treat every recipient with the utmost respect and honour. You have been placed in a position of trust and now, in spiritual terms, you will be giving a cup of water (a refreshing word) to a person who belongs to the Messiah and He promises that you will surely be rewarded. "The LORD God has given me the tongue of the learned, that I should know how to speak a word in season to him who is weary." Even spiritual giants might be lacking in an area, but when you speak the word in season, he or she will be enriched and fed by God's word that you're delivering on His behalf. Just remain faithful: "Each morning He awakens my ear to hear like those who are taught." If you are unclear, then take a step back and ask Him to confirm the word or to elaborate on it; have I got it all? Am I missing anything or any detail? Do I understand how you want me to pass Your word on? Is it the right time? The spirit of the prophet is subject to the prophet and God's gifts (words as well) are without repentance, which means, He's not going to snatch it away from you; on the contrary, He implores you here to be thorough and make sure you don't withhold anything that should enrich and comfort the recipient of His word. You cannot be judgemental. Here He will plead the cause of the other person and will require an answer from you if you give the message in a biased way. Take good care of His Body, your family, as you speak His words unto them, for if one part of the body suffers, the whole body suffers. But don't let overcautiousness hinder you; take your place in Him and just speak His truth in love. Both of you will then find the joy of an apt word in God.

Almighty God and heavenly Father, Lord Jesus Christ, Holy Spirit; help me to see each person I have a word for as You see them; to truly prophesy out of Your eyes and mouth, in Jesus' name, amen.

Own notes:

Day 3

Prophecy: merciful, gracious, slow to anger

> Do not associate (make no friendships) with a man given to anger; or go with a hot-tempered man, or you will learn his ways and find yourself caught in a trap (endanger your soul). You might learn their habits and not be able to change. TM: Don't hang out with angry people; don't keep company with hotheads. Bad temper is contagious – don't get infected.

Anger is defined as extreme displeasure. God is slow to anger, and we should be too. When the LORD gets angry, He will have seen the whole situation perfectly. That's why we read of Him, "The LORD is merciful and gracious, slow to anger and abounding in mercy." And, "The LORD is gracious and full of compassion, slow to anger and great in mercy." Human anger, particularly people who are prone to it, short-fused people, are born from an exaggerated sense of self; it can be a fruit of envy, pride, self-righteousness, judgemental attitudes and a sense of entitlement. Anger has inherent power and will move people to speak or act without thinking things through. We should never entertain anger or envy when we prophesy. Jonah was angry at the LORD once the LORD gave Nineveh another chance to repent. "But it displeased Jonah exceedingly, and he became angry. He knew that the LORD is a gracious and merciful God, slow to anger and abundant in loving kindness, one who relents from doing harm." When we prophesy, we will regularly see God's mercy, grace and love abounding; we will see His compassion far more than the "justice" we would require ourselves. Jesus sternly rebuked James and John for wanting to command fire to come down from heaven to consume His adversaries. He dissociated Himself from their attitude and refused to participate in their anger. God's not willing that any should perish, but that all should come to repentance. That's an important principle in prophecy – His voice is not about condemnation, but of restoration, healing, edification, comfort and, if necessary, repentance. Slow to anger, rich in mercy, full of grace and kindness; that's godly prophecy, that's the mind of God!

Almighty God and heavenly Father, Lord Jesus Christ, Holy Spirit; help me to choose my companions well, help me to be part of a healthy spiritual network; godly people who love You and are able to help me to be a tremendous blessing to them, in Jesus' name, amen.

Own notes:

Day 4
Of myself I cannot say or do anything

> Don't be one of those who give pledges, guaranteeing loans (debts) made to others; for if you don't have the wherewithal to pay, they will take your bed away from underneath you. NLT: Don't promise to be responsible for someone else's debts. If you should be unable to pay, they will take away even your bed.

"You know the generous grace of our LORD Jesus Christ. Though He was rich, yet for your sakes He became poor, so that by His poverty He could make you rich." Now enriched by Him, you're called to be His envoy or messenger. You can speak on His behalf, but never stand guarantee for something you don't have the power or authority to back up. A bit like a postman, deliver the letter, faithfully, and most often that's it. Even though our intentions might be good and very sympathetic, unless the LORD's in it, we cannot personally back it up. Don't take up issues out of good principle; don't fight battles that's not yours to fight. You can't take responsibility for everyone, not even Jesus did that in His earthly walk. God has designated each one of us a sphere of influence (cf. 2 Cor. 10:13). We can and should never act independently from this important fact. Both Moses and Paul wanted to sacrifice *themselves* to see the nation of Israel saved, but God would not allow it; only He could pay their debt, as noble as it was, as they didn't have the means to pay for their nation's debt.

Still, we can persuade the One who can, when we "make up the hedge" in people's lives; as His kings and priests, we can effectively intercede on their behalf and see them enjoy breakthroughs in the LORD. As ambassadors, we take the word of the LORD to His people, but we also bring them before the LORD, whether to intercede for them or to bless them from a heavenly position. We never come with persuasive words of human wisdom, i.e. in our own strength, but we deliver God's messages in the demonstration of Holy Spirit and power. *He* backs up *His* word. Do it in your own strength, and they'll take away your bed, you will lose your place of rest!

Almighty God and heavenly Father, Lord Jesus Christ, Holy Spirit; thank You for the ability to speak on Your behalf; help me to know my sphere and operate effectively in it with You. Thank You that we sit together in the strategy rooms of heaven, dispensing blessings to Your people; help me to be a good envoy for You, in Jesus' name, amen.

Own notes:

Day 5

Establishing boundaries as God willed it

> Do not move the ancient (everlasting) boundary (border, landmark) which your fathers have set (established). NLT: Don't cheat your neighbour by moving the ancient boundary markers set up by previous generations.

This is such an important principle and it ties in with the previous proverb. "You shall not move your neighbour's boundary mark, which the ancestors have set, in your inheritance which you will inherit in the land that the LORD your God gives you to possess" (Deut. 19:14). In plain English it's saying, "Don't stealthily encroach on someone else's field of ministry as determined by the LORD and His people." Boundaries designate the limits to a territory possessed by someone, or to the one who has to oversee and manage it. In both the OT and in the NT we see God set boundaries for the tribes of Israel and for whole nations (tribal as well as ethnic) (cf. Num. 21:13; Deut. 3:16). In the NT, Paul stated the same: "And He has made from one blood every nation of men to dwell on all the face of the earth, and has determined their pre-appointed times and the boundaries of their dwellings." This is all literal and in the natural, but also true in the spirit. When we prophesy, we need to recognise this. Don't encroach on someone else's patch; don't try and cover or take ownership of an area or people that was not designated to you. Especially when you think you could do better! Cultivate *your* field, make it abundantly fruitful for the LORD. Father is very clear about it, and it ties in with your appointed sphere of influence. Don't add any words you think should go with His message and don't detract any either. Sow what you need to sow where He's told you to sow; anything else is outside His will and purpose and it will cost you dearly in the end. The "fathers" here shows that the Body will only allow you to operate in a sphere they can accept; right or wrong, even when you know you are right, stick to their authority, for in the end, it is a matter between them and the LORD – you just speak His word or message faithfully. Stay safe, stay where He appointed you, and give no foothold to the devil or man.

Almighty God and heavenly Father, Lord Jesus Christ, Holy Spirit; thank You for my spiritual fathers and help me to father Your children well, help me to instil in them good boundaries and a thorough understanding of Your grace, love and destiny for them, in Jesus' name, amen.

Own notes:

Day 6

And then you'll stand before kings ...

> Do you see a man diligent and skilled in his work? He will stand before kings; He will not stand before obscure men. Do you see a man skilled at (who excels in) his work? He will serve kings, not obscure people. TM: Observe people who are good at their work – skilled workers are always in demand and admired; they don't take a back seat to anyone.

These prophetic principles are all excellent! Here, Father encourages you to hone your prophetic gift, craft it, pray about it, mature in it and get good at it, for when you do, He'll set you before nobility. He will trust you with high ranking information and send you to His kings and priests to bring His message and to perform His will. You can only excel in your work when you are secure in your identity and office in the LORD, and when you have the confidence and integrity to follow His leading. Whatever you then say will be in accordance to His will and guidance, then victory, success and breakthroughs will follow. The mainstay is faithfulness, because of your love for Him and His people. Dedicated to serve Him well, devoted to follow Him step by step and to be meticulous in doing His will as He leads you moment by moment. We do "what is right", never losing heart, endeavouring to complete His will no matter what circumstances we face. Obedient to the hilt, for He has prepared us to do "good works" in Him, motivated by love. Primarily, here, to convey His heart and will skilfully to others. "For the [true] love of God is this: that we do His commands [keep His ordinances and are mindful of His precepts and teaching]. And these orders of His are not irksome (burdensome, oppressive or grievous)." He also promises that once we show ourselves approved in the smaller assignments, and show due care how we prophesy and to whom we prophesy, the assignments will become more and more important. The most important King you'll then face and whose company you'll enjoy is of course, the LORD Himself.

Almighty God and heavenly Father, Lord Jesus Christ, Holy Spirit; teach me continuously how to be better at representing You, in Person, in love and in truth, in Jesus' name, amen.

Own notes:

Day 7
Entertain God's guests and serve them well

> When you sit down to dine with a ruler, consider carefully (note well) what is before you, and put a knife to your throat if you are a man of great appetite (gluttony). Do not desire his delicacies, for it is deceptive food. NLT: While dining with a ruler, pay attention to what is put before you. If you are a big eater, put a knife to your throat; don't desire all the delicacies, for he might be trying to trick you.

James wrote, "Happy is the person who remains faithful under trials, because when he (or she) succeeds in passing such a test, he will receive as his reward the life which God has promised to those who love Him. If you are tempted by such trials, we must not say, "This temptation comes from God." For God cannot be tempted by evil, and He Himself tempts no one. But we are tempted when we are drawn away and trapped by our own evil desires." It's thus highly unlikely that "the ruler" is referring to the LORD. In fact, the most logical "ruler" here is the person you were sent to serve, in terms of giving a prophecy or message from God. That word should be the Bread of Life from the LORD to that person. Sitting down and eating with him or her would be to try and digest what was given to *them*. Don't try to be clever and participate too much, making yourself so at home that you forget who you are, and why you are there. At times, we can be so excited for people that we draw attention to ourselves instead of keeping the focus, as God intended, on the recipient. The test is to remain sensitive to what the LORD wants to say and then within that fellowship remain within that culture of honour and humility. The prophecy itself (the food supplied) is the test. Are you making more of it than you should be? Are you drawing out of the prophetic realm more than was intended? Be careful, just pass on what was given and remain faithful as His envoy; always remember – familiarity breeds contempt. The world with all its desires will pass away, but he that does the will of the LORD will abide forever.

Almighty God and heavenly Father, Lord Jesus Christ, Holy Spirit; You are my desire, You'll feed and provide for me, help me to submit to Your will and authority in humble obedience. You alone can satisfy my hunger and thirst for You. In Jesus' name, amen.

Own notes:

Day 8

My Beloved is mine and I am His

> Do not weary yourself (labour) to gain wealth; be smart enough to desist (cease) if you make your eyes rush at it, when you set your eyes on it, it is gone. For wealth certainly makes itself wings like an eagle that flies towards the heavens. TM: Don't wear yourself out trying to get rich; restrain yourself; riches disappear in the blink of an eye; wealth sprouts wings and flies off into the wild blue yonder.

This seems to be addressed to the workaholic, one pursuing worldly money and riches. Instead, Jesus taught, "Do not lay up for yourselves treasures on earth, where moth and rust destroy and where thieves break in and steal; but lay up for yourselves treasures in heaven… for where your treasure is, there your heart will be also." In the spiritual sense, although we are encouraged to be zealous of the best spiritual gifts, for they truly enrich us, we are exhorted to earnestly pursue love. What are the riches that can never be destroyed? Tongues will cease; prophecy, understanding and knowledge without love is "nothing". So, what is Father endeavouring to teach us here? Concerning life and the prophetic life, in particular? The gift itself, the ability to speak on His behalf, is not our pursuit as a prophetic people; we speak *because* we love, we don't speak to obtain more from the LORD. It's not about the riches that accompany great anointings or divine gifts, it's always about

God Himself, and our love for Him and for our (His) family. Our response to the assignment should be, "Father-God, this word I carry as a great treasure, on Your behalf, to the person You love, and I love in You." If the riches and spiritual wealth you enjoy because you can flow in His gifts become the prime motivator, you will be left poor at the end of the day. You will seek recognition and validation, which is so much part of the orphaned heart. But if You can pass on great blessing without receiving anything but the LORD's approval, then You will remain eternally rich. He will make sure you are rewarded, but it will be in His time and in His way. Your identity is not wrapped up in your gifts or anointings; it's in your character as a child of God.

Almighty God and heavenly Father, Lord Jesus Christ, Holy Spirit; You are my richest blessing, You in Person, it is You I love and love to follow; help me to bring You honour and glory when I minister in Your precious name, in Jesus' name, amen.

Own notes:

Day 9

Bless others without any hidden motives

> Do not eat the bread of a selfish (miserly, stingy) man, or desire his delicacies; for as he thinks within himself, so he is. He says to you, "Eat and drink!" But his heart is not with you. You will vomit up the morsel you have eaten, and waste your compliments. NLT: Don't eat with people who are stingy; don't desire their delicacies. They're always thinking about how much it costs. "Eat and drink," they say, but they don't mean it. You will throw up what little you've eaten, and your compliments will be wasted.

Here we see the sharp contrast between God's kingdom of light and Satan's kingdom of darkness within this world. In his quest for dominion, Lucifer exclaimed full of pride, "I will" five times. In his own kingdom, he stood to gain independence and self-determination; it's about "I, me and myself"; such selfishness is driven by want and greed. "Your rich commerce led you to violence, and you sinned... Your heart was filled with pride because of all your beauty. Your wisdom was corrupted by your love of splendour... You defiled your sanctuaries with your many sins and your dishonest trade." And, "by your great wisdom in your trade you have increased your wealth, and your heart has become proud in your wealth." He always had an ulterior motive. Jesus declared of him, and those who align themselves with him, as not caring for God's sheep, but they act like a thief and a robber. His ways remain the same: to entice and deceive. He pretended to be Eve's friend, but his heart was not with them: they ate together and sin entered their world. And still he offers mankind his deadly delicacies. Not so with Father-God. His kingdom is quite the opposite: what He says is what you get. The delicacy He offers is His Son, the Bread of Life. Partaking of Him brings life, peace, joy and abundant grace. God is sincerely generous. In terms of flowing prophetically, be sincerely generous too; don't have any ulterior motives, but love the ones you feed in His name; give generously, without expecting back. And you will prosper. God's food are real treats, and very fulfilling.

Almighty God and heavenly Father, Lord Jesus Christ, Holy Spirit; You are the Bread of Life indeed and when I live off You, I thrive. Help me to discern the deceptions and deceit of the enemy and those who adhere to his miserly and prideful ways, in Jesus' name, amen.

Own notes:

Day 10

A time to speak forth and a time to be quiet

> Do not speak in the hearing of a fool, for he will despise (scorn) the wisdom (good sense) of your words. NLT: Don't waste your breath on fools, for they will despise the wisest advice. GN: Don't try to talk sense to a fool; he can't appreciate it. TM: Don't bother talking sense to fools; they'll only poke fun at your words.

Remember Prov. 1:7? "The fear of the LORD is the beginning of knowledge, but fools despise wisdom and instruction." In our priestly prophetic function, we are dissuaded from prophesying to people who disregard God, or who'll disregard His word through *you*. He desires that none of our words will fall to the ground, but that they will accomplish the task whereunto they are sent. This is a great pearl of wisdom. God does not necessarily have a word of wisdom, knowledge or prophetic utterance for every single person you meet. Proclamation does *not* have to follow all revelation. God has discernment, and we should learn it too. Jesus spoke out strongly on this principle: "Don't waste what is holy on people who are unholy. Don't throw your pearls to pigs! They will trample the pearls, then turn and attack you." Believe it or not, obedience might be to remain silent at times, even if the LORD is using you mightily in speaking forth His mind. In this school, we would be wise to take this to heart. The right word might mean no word at all, and having the freedom to say, "I don't have a word from the LORD for you, but I'll continue to pray for you." God is always at work, but if we speak out of turn, we intrude on His plans for that person or persons. "Do not awaken love until it is ready." The incorruptible seed entrusted to us is precious; let us exercise discernment when and where to plant, according to His will and purpose. Discern when to speak and when not to speak to people. The letter kills, but the Spirit (the empowered word) gives life. That's the essence of prophecy, to be an accountable envoy and messenger for our great and glorious King.

Almighty God and heavenly Father, Lord Jesus Christ, Holy Spirit; I desire greatly to walk in sensitivity to You, to listen carefully and to speak responsibly all the time. Let me speak Your words in season and convict me when to be quiet, in Jesus' name, amen.

Own notes:

Day 11
Stand with God as He fights for the fatherless

> Do not move the ancient boundary or encroach onto the fields of the fatherless, for their Redeemer is strong; He will plead their case (take up their fight) against you. NLT: Don't cheat your neighbour by moving the ancient boundary markers; don't take the land of defenceless orphans. For their Redeemer is strong; He Himself will bring their charges against you.

There are four types of people to take special care of and endeavour never to short-change them; the widow, the fatherless, the stranger and the poor. Earlier we defined the fields of our lives by boundaries that were set before we could determine them. The mere fact that we can move them means that we have the capacity to expand on what has originally been assigned to us. Even in a literal sense, Paul wrote, "God decided beforehand when they [nations] should rise and fall, and He determined their boundaries." This was also true of Israel, as territory was allotted to each tribe. We know that this also equates to our own spiritual "sphere of influence". In the Greek, sphere or *kanon* means "a definitely bounded or fixed space within the limits of which one's power of influence is confined". The theological term probably refers to delegated authority. Because of our gifts and our anointings we also have a functional authority. We can do things well in certain areas: some are very good at prayer or preaching or administration; Paul calls them "graces". "Since we have gifts that differ according to the grace given to us, each of us is to exercise them accordingly." Even when we are "better" at some things than those who still struggle at finding their own feet, we are called to come alongside them, strengthen their borders, not to take over or rob them from their ability or authority to complete their tasks. The "fatherless" are also those who feel insecure, marginalised and rejected within the Body of Christ, not orphan-hearted, but vulnerable. When we prophesy, we must make sure we build them up, strengthen their claims in the kingdom and see them rise up and take their rightful place in Father's kingdom. Own your own land and help your neighbour to be fruitful in his designated realm.

Almighty God and heavenly Father, Lord Jesus Christ, Holy Spirit; when I take possession of the land You have allotted to me, let me do so without encroaching on or taking my neighbour's land, in Jesus' name, amen.

Own notes:

Day 12
Don't refuse criticism; get all the help you can

> Apply your heart (mind) to discipline (instruction) and your ears to words of knowledge. NLT: Commit yourself to instruction; listen carefully to words of knowledge. GN: Pay attention to your teacher and learn all you can. TM: Give yourselves to disciplined instruction; open your ears to tested knowledge.

Basic principles in our relationship with God is our ability to hear from Him and to be discerning in our walk with Him. It should be accompanied with the right attitude and a willingness to quickly obey. To be God's spokesperson we must apply our hearts to His instruction (discipline). The word "apply" here is active, "to come in", "to enter", implying we should "invite" God's discipline and instruction. Both David and the writer of Hebrews makes the same link: "Today if you hear His voice, do not harden your hearts, because of unbelief (disobedience)." God's will for us is to rest in His finished work and to hear His word, which will penetrate every part of our beings. But it starts by zealously pursuing Him, to exert ourselves to enter His glorious rest for us. It is out of that rest that we prophesy; out of a life of love, faith and obedience. Our teacher? Holy Spirit Himself! "The spirit of truth will guide you into all truth... whatever He hears, He will speak." And, "the anointing which you received from Him abides in you. His anointing teaches you about all things, and is true ... and just as it has taught you, you abide in Him." Holy Spirit is keen to renew us, to transform us by God's grace, to become the people we were always created to be, to encounter our own destiny in Him. For that to happen, we have to "apply" our hearts and "commit" to His discipline and discipling. There are so many voices speaking to us all the time. We must nurture the ability to pick out His voice, and that means listening out for Him. Taking the necessary time out to find Him, to "let go and let God", to tune into His frequency or spontaneous flow and to receive His word. Then write it down, capture His words, for they are life-giving and life-changing. He is waiting for you to draw near; will you go and wait *on* Him today?

Almighty God and heavenly Father, Lord Jesus Christ, Holy Spirit; sharpen my ability to hear from You day by day, make me alert and vigilant to respond quickly to Your inner prompting, in Jesus' name, amen.

Own notes:

Day 13

As His child, submit to His hand of correction

> Do not withhold discipline from a child; if you strike him with a rod, he will not die. You will strike him with the rod and rescue (save) his soul from Sheol. NLT: Don't fail to discipline your children. The rod of punishment won't kill them. Physical discipline may well save them from death. GN: A good spanking won't kill them. As a matter of fact, it may save their lives.

This is a vivid picture of a child resisting the admonishing of his or her parents. A disobedient, rebellious child who is disregarding all correction and rebukes. In the literal, the proverb advocates corporal punishment as a deterrent for further misdemeanours and as an important tool to help a child to develop protective boundaries. The parents must set clear guidelines for their child for healthy living, with God, themselves, the family, and the wider community. If the child learns to respect the set lines or boundaries, and knows it's is done in love, then it will help that child in the long run to avoid pitfalls and even correction by society itself and/or drifting into a life of lawlessness, which will ultimately lead to death. This is also true in spiritual terms. So, we need God's correction in our life. "My son, do not make light of the LORD's discipline, and do not lose heart when He rebukes you, because the LORD disciplines the one He loves, and He chastens everyone He accepts as His son. Endure hardship as discipline; God is treating you as His children. For what children are not disciplined by their father?... Submit to the Father of spirits and live in order that we may share in His holiness. No discipline seems pleasant at the time, but painful. Later on, however, *it produces a harvest of righteousness and peace.*" The rod represents God's word. That word can come in many forms, but it is best when we hear it immediately and respond in humility. Then we'll prophesy life and not death. This also ensures that in our short lives we'll be adequately prepared by Him for eternity. When you then speak on His behalf, you will speak as one refined by fire, the fire of His sincere love.

Almighty God and heavenly Father, Lord Jesus Christ, Holy Spirit; I submit to Your parenting and Your loving care; do whatever is necessary to set proper spiritual boundaries in my life, in Jesus' name, amen.

Own notes:

Day 14

Born to speak at such a time as this

> My son, if your heart is wise, my own heart also will be glad; and my innermost being (kidneys) will rejoice when your lips speak what is right. NLT: My child, if your heart is wise, my own heart will rejoice! Everything in me will celebrate when you speak what is right. GN: My child, if you become wise, I will be very happy. I will be proud when I hear you speaking words of wisdom. TM: My heart will dance and sing to the tuneful truth you'll speak.

Amazing! When we are in tune with Father-God's heart and speak forth His words as He desires, God rejoices! Greatly rejoices. What incentive to be His prophetic kings and priests. Knowing Him and understanding His mind, flowing with His plans, then, speaking His heart or mind. God wants us to be wise. He loves it when we seek out His heart and understand His wisdom, as encapsulated in Jesus. Then we can effectively represent Him and His kingdom – we can minister Life and Truth and show the way to a broken world and fellow believers. That's authentic prophecy, coming from a heart that excites and gladdens God! He, Almighty God, in His innermost being rejoices and celebrates when we speak what is "right". That motivates us to speak His "in-tune truth" that will make His heart dance. When a sinner repents, heaven rejoices; when we prophesy wisely, as God intends and desires, He *greatly* rejoices (heaven with Him too? Probably!). Let's recap; it starts with your identity and calling, knowing who you are in Him (the boundaries), let Him be your passion, don't be deceived, only speak to the one God sends you to; always keep God's aims in sight, be open to God's correction and now, aim to get it "right" – become thoroughly acquainted with Jesus and abide in Him. Out of that deep, deep personal relationship with Him, God wells up His love, His life and His words for and through you. Your destiny is manifested in the uniqueness of time, now. God had *you* in mind for today, so that He would deploy His plans in this world. As we yield to Him and as we commune with Him, making time for Him, we are, at the same time, changed inside out; to speak on His behalf and see great things happen, but above it all, to see Him rejoice.

Almighty God and heavenly Father, Lord Jesus Christ, Holy Spirit; I submit to You in love, guide me to speak the right word at the right time in the right way for I desire to make Your heart "sing and dance" in Jesus' name, amen.

Own notes:

Day 15
Having done all, enabled to stand with Him (Eph. 6:13)

> Don't let your heart envy sinners, but continue in (be zealous for) the fear of the LORD all day long; for then you will have a future; and your hope will not be cut off. GN: Don't be envious of sinful people; let reverence for the LORD be the concern of your life. If it is, you have a bright future. TM: Don't for a minute envy careless rebels; soak yourself in the fear of God; that's where your future lies.

This is also profound. When you prophesy, you must grasp, comprehend and embrace your own position in God. You cannot look at people, their circumstances, assets *or* wrongdoings for that matter. Know where you are, as you deliver the message; you are in the constant presence of Almighty God, for even as His envoy, you are never without Him or His scrutiny. The eyes of the LORD are ever upon us. In the Biblical sense, envy means you want what others have, and jealousy is to be zealous for what others have; in the main, both are ungodly. Consider the paradoxes in the book of Ecclesiastes: "The fastest runner doesn't always win the race, and the strongest warrior doesn't always win the battle. The wise sometimes go hungry, and the skilful are not necessarily wealthy." David had great difficulty in reconciling the successes of the wicked, but once God showed Him His side of things, he changed his mind (cf. Psa. 73): "Then I went into your sanctuary, O God, and I finally understood the destiny of the wicked. Truly, you put them on a slippery path and sent them sliding over the cliff to destruction. In an instant they are destroyed, completely swept away by terrors." How awful! If you are going to be very effective in representing God it is of the utmost importance to see and understand your position in, but also before Him. Standing in reverential awe and respect for Him, yet knowing how completely He loves you and others. Paul wrote, "We serve God whether people honour us or despise us, whether they slander us or praise us. We love the truth." The fear of the LORD with a heartfelt passion for Him will make you an excellent messenger for Him!

Almighty God and heavenly Father, Lord Jesus Christ, Holy Spirit; You are my desire, it is Your face I seek, and when I speak on Your behalf, grant me the immediate awareness of Your presence with me. In Jesus' name, amen.

Own notes:

Day 16
Stay on course and don't get distracted

> Listen, my son, and be wise, and direct (guide, keep) your heart on the right path (way). Do not associate (join) with winebibbers; nor among gluttonous eaters of meat, for the drunkard and the glutton shall come to poverty, and drowsiness shall clothe a man with rags. My child, listen and be wise. Keep your heart on the right course. Do not carouse with drunkards or feast with gluttons, for they are on their way to poverty, and too much sleep clothes them in rags.

When we are urged to "hear" or "listen" and be wise, we should sit up and take special note. Father-God's themes here are about the kind of fellowship you keep and the need to exercise self-control. Stay on course, don't get distracted by worldly appetites, stay focused on the race and its destination. Keep your eyes firmly fixed on Jesus, our Champion who initiates and perfects our faith. The allure is to drink too much "wine" with others who indulge. Wine makes you lose touch with reality and drop your inhibitions. In the natural, life becomes virtual and distant, and problems and pain seemingly disappear for a time. But when you come to, you still have to face up to the same issues or problems in your life; often with a headache, regret and loss of valuable time. Basically, it refers to anything that gives you a high, that's intoxicating. A little is fine, but when it becomes excessive or addictive, it becomes destructive. It could be as simple as sport, music, leisure or even working *for* the LORD, instead of with Him. Wine's not the issue; it's the excess and the company it keeps. On a higher level, Holy Spirit's influence is likened unto wine. If we pursue spiritual things beyond what God intends for us, chasing after spiritual experiences and the feelings that accompany them, then this principle also becomes applicable. Gluttony, or overeating, is similar; some Christians, even some theologians, gorge themselves with information and a thorough analysis of the Scriptures, without being in relationship with Holy Spirit. They analyse for the sake of analysing and are "puffed up", rather than reflecting the truth and power that comes from God's Word. They grow fat on spiritual matters without regarding the portion *God* had dished up for them. Slumbering refers to living in your own dreamworld, and seeking one's own righteousness will leave you with spiritual rags. No, be wise and stay on God's path; walk humbly *with* your God and follow His lead.

Almighty God and heavenly Father, Lord Jesus Christ, Holy Spirit; help me to exercise self-control, help me to find Your path and stay on it, in Jesus' name, amen.

Own notes:

Day 17
Honour your father and mother...

> Listen to your father who gave you life (begot you), and do not despise your mother when she is old. GN: Listen to your father; without him you would not exist. When your mother is old, show her your appreciation. TM: Listen with respect to the father who raised you, and when your mother grows old, don't neglect her.

God is our Father, and so many Scriptures allude to this; Jesus is God, but in a mystery He is also God's begotten Son. And we are predestined to "become conformed to the image of His Son, so that Jesus would be the firstborn among many brethren". In Him we have also been adopted by Father-God, by the Spirit of adoption: "See how great a love the Father has bestowed on us, that we would be called children of God." And, "Everyone who believes that Jesus is the Christ (Messiah) has become a child of God. And everyone who loves the Father loves His children, too." Even in the OT, God declared His love as our "Father"; "I am your Father, and I have loved you ever since you were a child." And David wrote, "A father of the fatherless and a judge for the widows, is God in His holy habitation." How often do we disregard the voice of the One who gave us life and who loves us? Jesus promised us, "I will not leave you as orphans; I will come to you." Now, Jesus' other title is *Eternal Father*, Mighty God, Wonderful Counsellor and Prince of Peace. We are fathered by God, the Trinity, we have open access to Father through Jesus by Holy Spirit. We must know the voice of God well, but then we must also hear, and take heed and obey Him in love and thankfulness. We honour our spiritual fathers too: "Appreciate your pastoral ("fathering") leaders who gave you the Word of God. Take a good look at the way they live and let their faithfulness and truthfulness instruct you." As far as our "mother" goes, those who nurture us through the covenant of Grace, i.e. the Church, grows "out of time". She becomes "old" and often does not function optimally; she might not walk in "present truth" – in short, she might become outdated. Then *still* love her and care for her. Always show honour. Children frequently outrun their parents. Always treasure and hold in high esteem the people of God, for He treasures every single person held in her, ever loving them.

Almighty God and heavenly Father, Lord Jesus Christ, Holy Spirit; thank You for being my Father, and thank You for Your Church, and Holy Spirit ministering to me through Her. Thank You for all of my family; I will honour and love them always, in Jesus' name, amen.

Own notes:

Day 18

By grace, purchase God's eternal blessings

> Buy truth, and do not sell it; also, get wisdom and instruction (admonition; discipline) and understanding (good judgement, discernment). GN: Truth, wisdom, learning and good sense – these are worth paying for, but too valuable for you to sell.

This proverb will link in with the next verse, but demands separate consideration also. Bear in mind that these sayings are to help us as His prophetic people. The previous one leaves us in no doubt that we are a family and we should honour, love and respect God and the rest of our family, no matter what. Now, we see that we are to "buy" or "purchase" spiritual assets. There is a "price" to be paid. Wisdom is personified in Jesus, so, if you want to purchase wisdom, it will cost you your life! You must lay down your life for Him. If you want to be a prophetic king and priest, count the cost; John writes, seemingly quoting this proverb: "I counsel you to buy from Me gold refined in the fire, that you may be rich; and white garments, that you may be clothed, that the shame of your nakedness may not be revealed; and anoint your eyes with eye salve, that you may see (gain revelation and illumination; to discern)." The gold tried by fire depicts our fiery trials and tribulation, instilling godly character, refining us. We "buy" from God Himself, but also from those who nurture us. Every fiery experience out of which we learn and receive grace to understand, to change, to grow, we must embrace and make our own. Don't dismiss pain, sorrow and testing as being solely from the Enemy or the world (even though *they* will do their utmost to rob us). Find God's wisdom in every step you take, identify His instruction and learn from it. Gain His understanding and discernment in all matters before speaking out on His behalf. That's our testimony. As His children, we know He is not aloof; He is close by, present in our suffering. We stand in garments of grace and freely receive His Anointing to see when we are willing to sacrifice all else, to pay the price for Him, equipping us for life eternal, with Him.

Almighty God and heavenly Father, Lord Jesus Christ, Holy Spirit; help me to purchase more and more gold, if that means more fire, then, according to Your will and purpose only, let it be. Let grace reign supreme in my life, as I accept Your garments of righteousness and more and more and more of You, Holy Spirit, in Jesus' name, amen.

Own notes:

Day 19

Get into the divine cycle of love

> The Father of the righteous will greatly rejoice; and he who fathers (begets) a wise son will be glad (delight) in him. Let your father and your mother be glad, and let her rejoice who gave birth to you. NLT: The father of godly children has cause for joy. What a pleasure to have children who are wise. So give your father and mother joy! May she who gave you birth be happy.

God has made it so easy for mankind to bring Him great joy. Jesus said, "This is the only work God wants from you. Believe in the one He has sent." We have been made completely righteous with God in Christ (cf. Rom. 5:17; 2 Cor. 5:21). We are the righteous children of God because we believe in Jesus Christ as our Saviour, Redeemer and Justifier. What gives Him more joy than seeing His children in love with Him and seeking to please Him? Searching His presence and wisdom, *and* finding it. To be a blessing unto Him and His kingdom. There can be no other objective but to live out a life reconciled unto Almighty God in love and humility, in faith and thankfulness, in hope and joy. Then starts the transformation, the metamorphosis, preparing you for an eternity with Him, but the schooling and nurturing is here while we sojourn upon the earth. This is where we learn to trust God and know His constant goodness in the face of any and all adversity, and that impartation of His divine character and holiness gives Him great joy. He sees the end, an eternal weight of glory. But there is also the aspect of honour, Paul writes to his spiritual children in Ephesus: "I, a prisoner for serving the LORD, beg you to lead a life worthy of your calling, for you have been called by God." "Behaviour that's a credit to the summons to God's service." There is a "good" or "divine cycle of love" here; as we spend time with God, appropriate our access by Holy Spirit and partake of His joy everlasting and pleasures evermore, we cause Him great joy! And as we bring Him more joy, we bubble up Holy Spirit (champagne) and bring joy and happiness to all those around us too.

Almighty God and heavenly Father, Lord Jesus Christ, Holy Spirit; my joy is to know You rejoice in and over me. Help me to make You proud of me; not by merit, but by my sincere and loving response to Your great love for me. My utmost for Your highest joy, in Jesus' name, amen.

Own notes:

Day 20
With joy, drink deeply from God's fountain

> My son, give me your heart and let your eyes observe (delight in) my ways, for a harlot (an adulterous woman) is a deep pit, and a foreign woman (wayward wife) is a narrow well. Like a bandit (robber) she lies in wait and multiplies (increases) the unfaithful (covenant breakers; treacherous) among men. TM: Dear child, I want your full attention; please do what I show you. A whore is a bottomless pit; a loose woman can get you in deep trouble fast. She'll take you for all you've got; she's worse than a pack of thieves.

These sayings are comprehensive. Father-God is warning us against impending dangers; how to foresee them and how to avoid them, protecting ourselves in Him. We are married to God (cf. Rom. 7:3; Eph. 5:25). Our covenant and intimacy with Him can be threatened by alluring, enticing distractions. The harlot represents all those things or opportunities that offers gratification or pleasure outside of God's will and desire for you. She offers water for your thirsts (urges), but her price is too high. Our feelings and thoughts dictate the way we act. It's not on the spur of the moment, but it is when our personal desires draw us away from His presence and covenantal relationship. Succumbing to any temporary gains for satisfaction, for self, excluding God and His person. It might even seem very pious and good. For instance, general prophecy *is* good, but if it is to prop yourself up or to gain acceptance from others, and not from the LORD Himself, you are also gratifying your own needs and desires. Don't be put off by this; in God's hands and from His heart, general prophecy can be very useful. It's about honouring Him and intimacy with Him will cultivate that. A deep well has less water to yield and requires harder work, so it will cost you a lot. Don't get distracted, but delight in the ways of God; tell Him your needs and bring it before Him in prayer, supplication and thanksgiving. Let go of all selfish ambitions and yield to His plan for you. The harlot is very good at what she does, so be on the outlook and avoid all of her temptations; don't drink from her cup, but rather seek God's wisdom and mind in all things and *so* you will prosper; drink from His well and He'll quench the thirst.

Almighty God and heavenly Father, Lord Jesus Christ, Holy Spirit; I want to be faithful to You in every step of my life. Help me to follow You alone and to discount any distractions, in Jesus' name, amen.

Own notes:

Day 21

His wine is always better than anything else

> Who has woe? Who has sorrow? Who has strife? Who has complaints? Who has needless bruises? Who has bloodshot eyes? Those who linger over wine, who go to sample bowls of mixed wine. Do not gaze at wine when it is red, when it sparkles in the cup, when it goes down smoothly! In the end it bites like a snake and poisons like a viper. Your eyes will see strange sights, and your mind will imagine confusing things. You will be like one sleeping on the high seas, lying on top of the rigging. "They hit me," you will say, "but I'm not hurt! They beat me, but I don't feel it! When will I wake up so I can find another drink?"

We were warned about illegal soul-ties and covenants, and now we are warned about self-indulgence and escaping spiritual reality. A lot of things can make us yearn for the intoxicating feeling that "new wine" can offer. But we must remain discerning, seeking *God's* wine at *His* table only. Isaiah warned Israel, "Woe to those who rise early in the morning to run after their drinks, who stay up late at night till they are inflamed with wine. They have harps and lyres at their banquets, pipes and timbrels and wine, but they have no regard for the deeds of the LORD, no respect for the work of His hands. Therefore, my people will go into exile for lack of understanding; those of high rank will die of hunger and the common people will be parched with thirst." Note the "linger longer", and "gazing into nothingness" and drinking "too much". We can enjoy a measure of our fruitfulness, "a feast is made for laughter and wine makes merry". But it becomes a problem when other things fill the gap that God and His presence should fill. Even when we dance and worship and rejoice, do we do it at the expense of what God wants to do at that moment? His reality. The sensationalism that accompanies some worship, preaching and ministering is worrisome at times. As a prophetic people, our access into the heavenly realm must be in line with what God's strategy dictates, not what *we* necessarily think and enjoy. Take a step back and always ensure He is still with you in *full* measure. God will never leave you or forsake you, but you will function with less power when you drift away from Him. No, draw near to God and He *will* draw near to you.

Almighty God and heavenly Father, Lord Jesus Christ, Holy Spirit; no carnality LORD please, and keep me from settling for plonk; rather help me to remain *filled* with Holy Spirit all the time, in Jesus' name, amen.

Own notes:

Day 22
Choose your friends well, and ask for God's help

> Don't envy evil (wicked) men, nor desire to be with them; for their minds devise (plot, are occupied with) violence, and their lips talk of trouble (their words always stir up trouble). GN: Don't be envious of evil people, and don't try to make friends with them. Causing trouble is all they ever think about; every time they open their mouth someone is going to be hurt.

Another core message of Proverbs is to "choose your companions well". We are often reminded along the lines of, "Bad company corrupts (ruins) good manners (character)." It is true in both literal and spiritual terms. A legalistic, critical person will soon get you to follow suit and soon you will take that same spirit behind his or her voice on board. When you are surrounded by tactless people, even those who prophesy (which is the theme here), their words will often tend to be hard and merciless. That's also why spiritual "tribes" and cultural ethos can influence us. Father-God wants us to be unbiased and pure in our delivery of His messages to His people. So, we are called to be discerning in our choices of people and we must quickly discern those who form weapons against God's plans, and those who accuse people in judgement. Why the envy? For these prophets wield power, but it is manipulative, legalistic and has self-gain in mind. The violence implies insensitivity and taking what's not theirs; even just doing so verbally, or their violence merely destroys what was intended for good. These orphan-hearted people will not show mercy or grace, which is another symptom of a violent heart. They are unforgiving and always call for justice and retribution. Their motives will ultimately mirror that of the father of lies, to steal, kill and destroy. "And in their greed (these false prophets) will exploit you with false words… they have their hearts trained in greed… they promise them freedom, but they themselves are slaves of corruption." The ability to access the spiritual realm is relatively easy, but what matters is the heart and attitude when such revelation comes. Holy Spirit must remain our guide, with the love of God our motivation and the honour of Jesus foremost in our minds. Show mercy, be God's diplomat, not judge, and keep company with people who will support and build your ministry according to God's will and love.

Almighty God and heavenly Father, Lord Jesus Christ, Holy Spirit; bring the right people across my path, and help me to be a good friend and companion to those You have chosen for me, in Jesus' name, amen.

Own notes:

Day 23

Jesus is our firm foundation

> By wisdom a house is built, and by understanding it is established (made secure); and by knowledge the rooms are filled with all kinds of costly (precious) and pleasant riches. NLT: A house is built by wisdom and becomes strong through good sense. Through knowledge its rooms are filled with all sorts of precious riches and valuables.

"Unless the LORD builds the house, they labour in vain who build it." As a prophetic people, we speak on behalf of God, we speak creatively, and we labour with Jesus (God's Wisdom personified) in building "houses". Note, we don't pull down, but build up; if there is rebuilding to be done, then we *assist* in rebuilding. Be careful, your godly gifts should not define you, but they should empower you to bless others. Your gifts will open doors for you and they will take you to the top of the mountain, but it will only be your character that keeps you there. Paul wrote similarly to the Corinthians, when he stressed that we are co-labourers of the Master-builder and we need to build with gold, silver and precious stones. Once it's built by Wisdom, like strong walls, our good sense, understanding and godly discernment should establish and secure us. How do we do it? When we receive the gift of Holy Spirit, He *is* God's grace (God-enablement; God-empowerment) to us. "The Spirit who dwells in us yearns for us" or "He's a fiercely jealous lover." He wants to fill our house (being) with His presence; His gifts and fruit to beautify *His* dwelling. We are the temple of Holy Spirit, and we must give Him full reign in our building; restoring and adorning our lives without restraint or interference from us. The doors must be open to Him, don't close it with things like selfish ambition or unforgivingness. Once our house is open to Him and being restored and beautified by Him, our prophetic words will impart that same process to those we speak to. That's true for those we prophesy to as well. There might be some cleaning out, but it's to redecorate according to God's "good plans" for that person. Then we'll be a holy habitation for Him.

Almighty God and heavenly Father, Lord Jesus Christ, Holy Spirit; be welcome in my own house, now it's Yours! Help me to build *with* You. Let me always co-labour with You in being a prophetic restorer. In Jesus' name, amen.

Own notes:

Day 24
Father will give you His Counsellor, His aide

> A wise man is strong (full of strength), and a man of knowledge increases (enhances) his might (power). For by wise guidance (clever strategy) you will wage war, and in abundance of counsellors (advisers) there is victory (deliverance). NLT: The wise are mightier than the strong, and those with knowledge grow stronger and stronger. So don't go to war without wise guidance; victory depends on having many advisers. TM: Strategic planning is the key to warfare; to win, you need a lot of good counsel.

The truly prophetic people always consult God in His strategy room. We have access through Jesus by Holy Spirit. Our wisdom comes from abiding in Jesus; He is our wisdom and strength. From the beginning of his ministry, Paul acknowledged his own inabilities and his complete reliance on Holy Spirit. "I came to you in weakness – timid and trembling. And my message and my preaching were very plain. Rather than using clever and persuasive speeches, I relied only on the power of the Holy Spirit. I did this so you would trust not in human wisdom but in the power of God." He is our prophetic source, He makes us "full of strength"; in addition, we increase our strength by consulting our divine counsellor before we make any decision or speak any words. We must get a vision of this: you have the Living God, Himself, indwelling you, you are empowered by grace to overcome, to be a witness for the King and His Kingdom. Such counsel and agreement includes your co-workers here in the world; "where two (or three because God's included!) agree about anything you ask for (an agreed strategy), it will be done for you by my Father in heaven." That's how we engage in all warfare, fully dressed and in agreement, not forgetting that prophecy forms part of your weapons of war (1 Tim. 1:18). Prophecy ushers in the victory, and it prepares God's people to accomplish His assignment for them. And when we receive a prophecy we must ensure an internal witness or consult with Holy Spirit, our divine counsellor, afterwards, clarify the prophecy, and seek His heart on the word He had given you. We must encourage people to take ownership of the prophecy for themselves. We're to be God's voice, messengers of godly counsel, to ensure God's victory in our lives as His kingdom people.

Almighty God and heavenly Father, Lord Jesus Christ, Holy Spirit; thank You for empowering me by Your grace, for without You I can do nothing, but with You I can do all things. You are my life and my love; make me the prophetic king and priest You've called me to be. In Jesus' name, amen.

Own notes:

Day 25

A fool can't be a counsellor; he lacks wisdom

> Wisdom is too exalted (high, lofty) for a fool, He does not open his mouth in [the assembly] at the gate. NLT: Wisdom is too lofty for fools. Among leaders at the city gate, they have nothing to say. Wise sayings are too deep for foolish people to understand. They have nothing to say when important matters are being discussed. TM: Wise conversation is way over the head of fools; in a serious discussion they haven't a clue.

"The message of the cross is foolish to those who are headed for destruction! But we who are being saved know it is the very power of God." Paul has a way with words, and he uses an oxymoron saying something similar. "Let no man deceive (fool) himself. If anyone among you thinks that he is wise by this world's standards (in this age), let him become a fool that he may become wise. For what this world considers wisdom is nonsense (foolishness) in God's sight. For it is written, 'God traps (catches) the wise in their cleverness (own craftiness).'" This principle carries through to the spiritual level, where we must engage with God's wisdom (Wisdom) when we face important matters. In fact, this proverb is quite severe: *if you don't know God's mind, you don't have anything to bring to the table!* His answers to our problems might often seem foolish to others, but when we are in an authentic relationship with Him, not matter how foolish His advice might seem, that's where the power of God brings salvation, deliverance and victory. For instance, "forgive *and* forget" is foolishness to the world, but extremely powerful in the kingdom. "God chose what the world looks down on and despises, and thinks it is nothing, in order to destroy what the world thinks is important." And, "whoever does not have the Spirit (a fool – not listening to Holy Spirit, even if only for the moment) cannot accept the things that come from the Spirit of God, for they are foolishness to him, and he cannot understand them, because they are spiritually discerned. The proverb also intimates that we should mostly prophesy to those who can discern, otherwise your words will fall on deaf ears. Something else: if you are wise, then you have a voice in God's gate; remember, your voice counts, so use it well!

Almighty God and heavenly Father, Lord Jesus Christ, Holy Spirit; thank You for giving me a voice, and help me to ensure that I am in tune with You before I speak on Your behalf; let my words be mighty, empowered by You, in Jesus' name amen.

Own notes:

Day 26

It's His plan, in His time and in His way

> Whoever plots evil will be known as a schemer (troublemaker). The devising of folly is sin, and people detest the scoffer (mocker) [he's an abomination to men]. GN: If you are always planning evil, you will earn a reputation as a troublemaker. Any scheme a fool thinks up is sinful. People hate a person who has nothing but scorn for others. TM: Fools incubate sin; cynics desecrate beauty.

Darkness cannot overcome light. The foolish plans of the wicked are destined to fail. A calculating person outside of God's strategy is dangerous, but he or she will eventually be exposed. Selfish ambition, pride and power-hungry people cannot succeed every time. Moses set a high standard: "But any prophet who fakes it, who claims to speak in my name something I haven't commanded him to say, or speaks in the name of other gods, that prophet must die. You may be wondering among yourselves, 'How can we tell the difference, whether it was God who spoke or not?' Here's how: If what the prophet spoke in God's name doesn't happen, then God wasn't behind it; the prophet made it up. Forget about him." However, the biggest schemer was Lucifer, the Devil. In his pride he schemed to rule over the darkness and set up his own kingdom. With his inflated sense of self-importance, he wanted to usurp authority not delegated to him, seeking undue honour and independence from God (cf. Isa. 14:12–15). His future? He was brought down low, down to the depths of the pit, condemned to the lake of fire for all eternity. We must be careful in our ability to see or hear, not to use it for our own advantage or for our own aims; nor seek recognition or try to gain subtle control. The easiest way to abuse one's gift is to become self-righteous; and mocking and accusations will follow such an attitude; the grace and mercy found in Jesus on the cross will then diminish, and such a person will also trample upon the grace found or sought by others. Controlling people often function out of "self", "I know better", and "thank God I'm not like them". They believe they "are" better than some; lacking humility and unable to show mercy. In your prophetic walk, don't do it your way, don't presuppose and don't deliver the word as *you* would want to give it. In all things, be wise, do it as Holy Spirit dictates, nothing more, nothing less and always full of mercy and grace.

Almighty God and heavenly Father, Lord Jesus Christ, Holy Spirit; I know the plans You have for me and those I prophesy to – plans to prosper, not to harm but to give me an expected end. Thank You. In Jesus' name, amen.

Own notes:

Day 27
Weak in a crisis? Weak indeed!

> If you falter in a time of trouble, how small is your strength? If you are slack in the day of distress, your strength is limited. NLT: If you fail under pressure, your strength is too small. GN: If you are weak in a crisis, you are weak indeed.

We have great assurance in the LORD. "Dear children, you are from God and have overcome them (everyone who works against the LORD), because He (God) who is in you is greater than the one who is in the world (our adversary)." Or, as TM put it, "You have already won a big victory over those false teachers, for the Spirit in you is far stronger than anything in the world." We walk with confidence and can only be caught off guard when we try to stand in our own strength. Whenever the day of distress comes upon us, all we have to do is ask, "LORD, what is your take on this?" In fact, James is clear about it; like the eagle we should relish the storms, for they make us stronger! Perhaps he had the same idea in mind: "Consider it a sheer gift, friends, when tests and challenges come at you from all sides. You know that under pressure, your faith-life is forced into the open and shows its true colours." Once we are at the mercy of people, circumstances, or the enemy, we can say like David, "When I was desperate, I called out, and God got me out of a tight spot. God's angel sets up a circle of protection around us while we pray." This proverb confirms that as pilgrims here we will have to face adversity from time to time, but we have the upper hand in Christ Jesus. "The tools of our trade aren't for marketing or manipulation (previous proverb!), but they are for demolishing that entire massively corrupt culture. We use our powerful God-tools for smashing warped philosophies, tearing down barriers erected against the truth of God, fitting every loose thought and emotion and impulse into the structure of life shaped by Christ. Our tools are ready at hand for clearing the ground of every obstruction and building lives of obedience into maturity." Confidence comes from flowing in and with Holy Spirit. It doesn't come on day one, it needs to be cultivated, prayed about and put into practice, then when the day or time of trouble comes, you will be ready! And you'll be more than a conqueror in Him.

Almighty God and heavenly Father, Lord Jesus Christ, Holy Spirit; thank You that I can still the storm and gain victory in every conflict, for Your power and shield is more than enough for me. In Jesus' name, amen.

Own notes:

Day 28
Speak up, there's no excuse!

> Deliver (rescue) those who are being led away (drawn) to death, hold back those who are staggering to slaughter. If you say, "Surely, we knew nothing about it," does He not consider it who weighs the hearts? And does He not know it who keeps your soul? And will He not render (repay) to man according to His work? NLT: Rescue those who are unjustly sentenced to die; save them as they stagger to their death. Don't excuse yourself by saying, "Look, we didn't know." For God understands all hearts, and He sees you. He who guards your soul knows you knew. He will repay all people as their actions deserve.

Jesus came to save, He is "Saviour", the one who brings people to safety in Him. One could argue that the fact that we are apportioned death with or in Adam is unjust, but the truth of the matter is, we are *all* sinners. Yet Jesus stepped in to rescue and deliver us, to justify us and make us righteous in God's sight. "For as by one man's disobedience many were made sinners, so also by one man's obedience many will be made righteous." God demonstrated His love towards us in that while we were still sinners, Christ died for us. God does not expect anything from us that He wasn't willing to do! God's will is that none should perish, but all come to repentance, come to faith in Jesus

Christ. You may want to stand by passively, but this proverb precludes that. "Now I am making you a watchman for God's people. Therefore, listen to what I say and warn them for me." We see people condemned to eternal spiritual death daily; and we must therefore speak up. You must enquire from the LORD *that word* that will set people free from the bondages of sin and of this world. We must address issues on His behalf for all people, God gave us great authority, in prayers, intercessions, declarations, prophecy and proclamations to change atmospheres and people's lives. Read the previous proverb again, then read this again, they belong together. We will all stand before Jesus one day, so let us be accountable in our calling as a prophetic kingdom of priests. We have the joy of plucking people out of the fire for Jesus, not only for salvation, but also when people are led astray by the enemy and the world. Speak up, there's no excuse now!

Almighty God and heavenly Father, Lord Jesus Christ, Holy Spirit; give me a heart for the lost, all the lost, both saved and unsaved. Let me be relentless in speaking the words of Life as You determine, in Jesus' name, amen.

Own notes:

Day 29

Plans to give you a future and a hope

> My son, eat honey, for it is good, Yes, the honey (dripping) from the comb is sweet to your taste; know that in the same way wisdom is sweet for your soul. If you find it, then there will be a future (prospect) your hope will not be cut off, and your hope will not be cut off. TM: Likewise knowledge, and wisdom for your soul – get that and your future's secured, your hope is on solid rock.

Honey is made by bees (small spiritual creatures) who work selflessly in a community to produce that golden, wholesome, sweet food. Honey must always be consumed fresh as it can ferment (Lev. 2:11). According to David, the perfect law of the LORD; His sure testimony; His right precepts; His pure commandments; His true judgements and the "clean" fear of the LORD is sweeter than honey and the drippings of the honeycomb (Psa. 19). What do we need to eat? "Man shall not live by bread alone, but by every word that proceeds from the mouth of God." We consume and assimilate and digest His revelation, wisdom, knowledge, understanding and ways. That divine dialogue, that's our sustenance. In another paradigm, Jesus is our Bread of Life. His words are spirit and they give life. And God Himself is "good", "sweet" and "empowering", imparting His thick "honey-love" to us. Now, consider that Jesus *is* the Word. We must ingest and digest Him; as David wrote, "How sweet are Your words to my taste! Yes, sweeter than honey to my mouth!" Such intimate knowledge and wisdom is sought after. "You will seek Me and find Me when you search for Me with all your heart. I will be found by you." Once acquired, you'll have a hope and a future, which will not disappoint, "because the love of God has been poured out within our hearts through the Holy Spirit who was given to us." Our inheritance is secure in Him. Yes, eat His honey and pursue Him always. Be filled and share that hope with others, speak life into people's lives, help them dream anew as you feed them God's wonderful honey.

Almighty God and heavenly Father, Lord Jesus Christ, Holy Spirit; Your love is sweet and You are wonderful. I will seek Your face all the days of my life, for in You alone I find eternal life. In Jesus' name, amen.

Own notes:

Day 30

Prophecy shouldn't bring ruin; rather, new life

> Do not lie in wait, O wicked man, against the dwelling of the righteous; do not destroy (raid, plunder) his resting place (home); for a righteous man falls seven times, and rises again, but the wicked stumble in time of calamity. NLT: Don't wait in ambush at the home of the godly, and don't raid the house where the godly live. The godly may trip seven times, but they will get up again. But one disaster is enough to overthrow the wicked. TM: Don't interfere with good people's lives; don't try to get the best of them. No matter how many times you trip them up, God-loyal people don't stay down long; soon they're up on their feet, while the wicked end up flat on their faces.

Even in a literal sense this is seen in Scripture; look at Joseph, for instance. His own brothers "plundered his house" (emotionally and spiritually also – his identity and dreams). Joseph was sold as a slave. He "got up" and became a godly servant leader in Potiphar's home. The owner's adulterous wife ambushed him also, and she then did violence to him (tried to violate him). The result? "They bruised his feet with shackles, his neck was put in irons." As God's anointed prophet leader, he got up again and won favour with the jailer. During that time, "the word of the LORD tested (refined) him"; he had to hold on to his prophetic promises and dreams. Then, "the king sent for him and released him; the ruler of peoples set him free." Through all of this, God was in control: "God sent a man (Joseph) ahead." So, don't raid people's houses by speaking evil of them, gossiping or plundering the goodness that they hold. In your prophecies, don't condemn, control, demean or rob others of their person and dignity. If you do, you might find eventually you are up against the LORD Himself! Don't try to overpower people with your prophecies, and don't usurp or undermine their authority in Christ. To the fallen, speak God's mind. However, if you're on the receiving end, listen to Micah: "Do not gloat over me, my enemies! For though I fall, I will rise again. I'm down, but I'm not out. Though I sit in darkness, the LORD will be my light. He'll turn on the lights and show me His ways. I'll see the whole picture and how right He is. I will be restored, but my enemies will be disgraced." God's words *are* for edification, exhortation and comfort.

Almighty God and heavenly Father, Lord Jesus Christ, Holy Spirit; thank You that You never give up on us, and thank You that I can trust You in the fire, the face of adversity, even when I have fallen, for You surround me with songs of deliverance and victory, in Jesus' name, amen.

Own notes:

Day 31
Don't judge, lest you be judged

> Do not rejoice (gloat) when your enemy falls, and do not let your heart be glad (rejoice) when he stumbles; or the LORD will see it and be displeased (disapprove), and turn His anger (wrath) away from him. GN: Don't be glad when your enemies meet disaster, and don't rejoice when they stumble. The LORD will know if you are gloating, and He will not like it; and then maybe He won't punish them.

A crucial point and it follows naturally from the previous proverb. Father-God warns us about desiring or trying to enforce "justice", enjoying to "cast a judgement" against someone, particularly in prophecy. No wonder we are to pray for our enemies and bless them. God is rich in mercy and full of grace; He wants us to also show mercy, to forgive and forget the wrongs our enemies have afflicted upon us. God hates *schadenfreude* – rejoicing and gloating in the demise and suffering of our enemies, no matter how "right" it might seem. A spirit of self-righteousness, bitterness and unforgivingness will insist on worldly justice. A steely or stony heart will insist on its inherent sense of "fairness", "passing sentence" and "punishment". It makes one the judge, jury and executioner. This proverb clearly states that in such cases, you take the issue out of God's hands, and He will take exception to that bitterness, unforgivingness and self-righteous arrogance. He then withdraws His hand from the situation and will actually take pity on their plight. People who pursue worldly justice have no or little understanding of mercy and grace. Godly justice is best demonstrated by Jesus. As they drove the nails into His hands, He said, "Father forgive them for they know not what they do." "Bless those who persecute you; bless, and do not curse… repay no one evil for evil (a tooth for a tooth)." And, "See that no one renders evil for evil (impute legal justice), but always pursue what is good, both for yourselves and for all." And, "Beloved don't avenge yourself, but rather let God do what's necessary, for Scripture says, 'I will take revenge, I will pay back says the LORD.'" Please reflect on Jesus' parable about the unforgiving servant, and nurture mercy (cf. Matt. 18:22–35). Always turn the other cheek and, if possible, help your fallen enemy up (prophetically) and bring them to a place of mercy and love, fully restored in Christ (cf. Gal. 6:1).

Almighty God and heavenly Father, Lord Jesus Christ, Holy Spirit; while I was an enemy, You died for me, let me be Your voice of mercy and love to all people, regardless of what they do, in Jesus' name, amen.

Own notes:

Day 32
Don't look around, say what you have to say

> Do not fret because of evildoers or be envious of the wicked; for there will be no future (prospect, hope) for the evil man; the lamp of the wicked will be put (snuffed) out. GN: Don't let evil people worry you; don't be envious of them. A wicked person has no future – nothing to look forward to.

The wicked, nasty or evildoers are those people who have a total disregard for God and His principles. Their actions aren't just about "not thinking about God" as with the fool, they impose their will and often it is associated with "bringing harm or calamity", being hostile to God. For the Christian, this would be about those times when the LORD told you to do something and your response was to disobey. In that instance, as with the unbeliever, it's not one who doesn't seek God, but rather one who defies Him and His intended way of life. In terms of spirituality, they have made this world their habitation, they thrive "under the sun" by following their own selfish ambitions and aims. They live for what they can gain and achieve, and *this world and its god* defines them; they actively pursue and control things like money, power and authority, qualifications, family life, health and pleasure. In short, achieving the "good life" at any cost, especially disregarding God. In short, acceptance and fulfilment from and in this world (often in line with the enemy's aim for them). Yet, God in His mercy, "gives His best – the sun to warm and the rain to nourish – to everyone, regardless: the good and bad, the nice and nasty." When we prophesy, we might be faced with such a person, and here, once again, we are urged to stay unbiased and to just give God's word unbiasedly, for their outcome is not in your hands. In fact, here, like Psa. 73, it seems like they are prospering in spite of their wicked endeavours. "Don't be envious"; their future is awful, so show them mercy. Just be content to please Father-God by faithfully delivering His message to everyone He sends you to and do so without prejudice. If Christians prosper in those areas and spiritually, rejoice with them; when unbelievers prosper more than you, remember you are a child of the living God, passing through; trust in Him and in His provision, and don't look around, look to Him. You have a future! You have everything to look forward to – an eternity with God's favour upon your life!

Almighty God and heavenly Father, Lord Jesus Christ, Holy Spirit; keep me focused on my assignment in You. You will always provide exactly what I need, so thank You, in Jesus' name, amen.

Own notes:

Day 33
Respect God's delegated authority

> My son, fear the LORD and the king; do not associate (join) with those who are rebellious (given to change), for their destruction (disaster, calamity) will rise suddenly, and who knows the ruin (calamities) that comes from both of them? NLT: My child, fear the LORD and the king. Don't associate with rebels, for disaster will hit them suddenly. Who knows what punishment will come from the LORD and the king?

This proverb works on different levels, depending on "the king". Why "my son" here? It emphasises our adoption and relationship with Father-God before highlighting our need for reverential awe and respect for God and the King. These proverbs come from God's Father-heart instructing us on His person, ways and mind. Out of that filial understanding and relationship we must also cultivate a healthy fear of the LORD, and know who He is; the one who indwells unapproachable light. Even though we are encouraged to come boldly within a bond of deep love, we need to come in worship, humility, reverence and honour of Almighty God. "What are human beings that you are mindful of them, mortals that you care for them? Yet you have made them a little lower than God, and crowned them with glory and honour." The king can also be *any* authority delegated to rule and reign over us: God Himself, spiritual leadership or even human government. "Everyone must submit to governing authorities. For all authority comes from God, and those in positions of authority have been placed there by God. So anyone who rebels against authority is rebelling against what God has instituted, and they will be held responsible. For the authorities do not strike fear in people who are doing right, but in those who are doing wrong… The authorities are God's servants, sent for your good… So you must submit to them, not only to avoid punishment, but also to keep a clear conscience, and because it's the right way to live." The same principle applies to our spiritual leader: "Be responsive to your pastoral leaders. Listen to their counsel. They are alert to the condition of your lives and work under the strict supervision of God. Contribute to the joy of their leadership." And then there is our King of kings, who lovingly demands our every breath, and when we disregard any of them, we do so at our own peril. Be humble, learn about godly submission and prosper.

Almighty God and heavenly Father, Lord Jesus Christ, Holy Spirit; when You call me to prophesy, help me to respect the lines and boundaries of authority You have put in place, in Jesus' name, amen.

Own notes:

Epilogue

My sincere thanks to you for your willingness to walk with Holy Spirit through this book. I pray that you have been very blessed by using this book and gain all that Father-God intended for you. I pray that your ability to hear from God will be greatly enhanced and that you will be able to prophesy freely in His wonderful name. In Jesus' name, amen.

Bibliography

JONES, ALFRED, *Dictionary of Old Testament Proper Names*. Samuel Bagster and Sons, 1856.

MOUNCE, WILLIAM D, *Complete Expository Dictionary of Old and New Testament Words*. Zondervan, Grand Rapids, Michigan, 2006.

NICHOLSON, WILLIAM, *Bible Student's Companion*. Pickering & Inglis, London.

VINE, W E, *Vine's Complete Expository Dictionary of Old and New Testament Words*. Thomas Nelson, Nashville, Tennessee, 1985.

von ALLMEN, J J, *Vocabulary of the Bible*. Lutterworth Press, London, 1958.

http://www.scripture4all.org/OnlineInterlinear/Greek_Index.htm

http://www.scripture4all.org/OnlineInterlinear/Hebrew_Index.htm